Serlins

The Mysterious and Haunting History of Murders, Ghosts, and Fortune Telling

In Redwood County and Minnesota

William Rose, age 31.
The man they had to hang twice.

Nobody owns life, but anyone who can
pick up a frying pan owns death.

William S. Burroughs 1914-1997

THE MYSTERIOUS AND HAUNTING HISTORY OF MURDERS, GHOSTS, AND FORTUNE TELLING

In Redwood County & Minnesota

Bless This Hat
Publishing, Minnesota

First Edition
First Printing, 2017
Book design by Adrian Lee
Cover design by Adrian Lee
Interior photographs provided by Adrian Lee and Patricia Lubeck reprinted with permission.
Bless This Hat Publishing, is a registered trademark.
Library of Congress Cataloging-in-Publication Data
Lee, Adrian, 1970–
The Mysterious and Haunting History of Murders, Ghosts, and Fortune Telling: in Redwood County and Minnesota
Adrian Lee. — 1st ed.
p. cm.
Includes bibliographical references.

ISBN-13: 978-1546320906
ISBN-10: 1546320903

Bless This Hat Publishing
AdrianLee.Author@yahoo.com
A percentage of the proceeds from this book will be going to the Southwestern Crisis Center non-profit organization.

Printed in the United States of America.

We can only judge the present by what is left to us from the past.

Patricia Lubeck grew up in a small town in southwestern Minnesota. After graduating high school she moved to California, where she earned her Bachelor's Degree from University of CA, Santa Barbara, majoring in anthropology, psychology, and sociology. Her favorite pastime is spent visiting historic sites and museums across the country. She developed a passion for history and spends many hours researching and documenting early crimes—specifically true crimes committed in the 1800s to 1900s in Southwestern Minnesota. Reading about these gruesome murders and unsolved mysteries keeps her awake into the wee hours of the morning. What causes anyone to commit a crime is always hard to determine. Most crimes never have a clear-cut ending and you're left with more questions than answers. Patricia Lubeck is constantly looking for answers—the important thing is to document the truth, if you can find it.

Adrian Lee is the founder of *The International Paranormal Society* and a member of the *Luton Paranormal Society* in England. He has studied history to the highest level at Kent University and London University, England. He has comprehensively investigated ghosts and paranormal activity all over the globe. He first came to Minnesota early in 2008 to work on several paranormal video productions, and spent two years working in Minneapolis as the national and international news correspondent for a live paranormal talk radio show on 100.3 KTLK. He currently hosts the only weekly paranormal news quiz show, *More Questions than Answers*, live every Friday on the Dark Matter Digital Radio Network. He now resides in Southwest Minnesota.

He has also written the following books: *Mysterious Midwest: Unwrapping Urban Legends and Ghostly Tales from the Dead; Mysterious Minnesota: Digging up the Ghostly Past at 13 Haunted Sites; How to be Christian Psychic: What the Bible says about Mediums, Healers, and Paranormal Investigators* and *Tales of a Pioneer Town: the Earliest Stories of Sauk Centre, Minnesota.*

Foreword

When I initially gained permission to paranormally investigate the Redwood Falls museum with my team, it was with the agreement that I would document the investigation and historical research I unearthed in a series of lectures. This would help to provide much needed funding for the non-profit *Redwood County Historical Society*, as well as raising the profile of the property and the history of the county—a chapter solely dedicated to the town of Redwood Falls and Redwood County will be found in my forthcoming book: *More Mysterious Midwest.*

It was then through working with Patricia Lubeck that I suggested curating an exhibition on the murders, mysteries, and hauntings of Redwood County and Minnesota. This would provide more opportunities for funding through ticket sales and the guidebook you are now holding.

As a historian and former president of the Sauk Centre and Area Historical Society, I am fully aware of the problems that beset local historical properties and locations. From the finding and keeping of volunteers to the raising of funding, where a random problem with the archaic plumbing or antediluvian structure can instantly place an impossible strain on limited resources.

Unfortunately we are in a period of our existence when our valuable leisure time is taken up with many attractions and possibilities—especially for the young. It is my hope that by introducing history through local murder mysteries and the haunting of Redwood County and Minnesota, that a fascination of the past may be achieved—who does not like to hear a murder mystery or a ghost story.

The smaller towns and homesteads that litter the plains of the Midwest are increasingly my pre-occupation. These are the locations that the public are less familiar with, within the canon of paranormal non-fiction. I want to investigate and learn about these new sites. I want to steer away from the same old regurgitated locations that seem to be found in every lazy paranormal-themed book. I wanted to emphasis that paranormal activity and history can exist outside of the clichéd haunted

over-commercialized buildings. And I want to be the first to experience it and document it!

I believe this exhibition to be the first of its kind anywhere in the country. I am unaware of any other exhibition that outlines the history of paranormal investigating, with artifacts and the evidence of hauntings. This combined with the darker history of Redwood County has provided a morbidly fascinating and oddly intriguing, educational experience. This history reflects a sometimes lawless and recidivist period where law enforcement was at best patchy, with limited resources and technology. Criminals could easily jump from train-to-train and be unknown and untraceable in the next county.

I want to emphasis that this exhibition is not about exploiting innocent victims, or promoting other religions or religious practices. Education is key, and the more we know the more we can be aware—we can only judge the present from what is left to us from the past.

Sales from this guide will benefit the Southwest Crisis Center. If you are a victim of abuse please call 800-376-4311.

Adrian Lee

The Potato Masher Murder

1867—Potato Masher used to bludgeon Gertrude Roehl, Sigel Township, Brown County

Constable Joseph Schnobrich was making his rounds on a bitterly cold day in late January 1867. He was in the vicinity of the Wilhelm Roehl farm when he noticed there wasn't any smoke coming out of the chimney. He'd heard Wilhelm had left for Mankato a few days previously, so he decided to check on the family. Schnobrich entered the home around noon, saw the stove was out, and saw four small children huddled together in bed under the covers; all dressed, except for their shoes. The constable asked the oldest boy, John, where his mother was and he said, "She's dead." "How did it happen?" asked the constable. The boy replied, "Andreas Schmidt killed her and threw her in the cellar." The children were loaded up in the sleigh and taken to a neighbor's house.

The constable and a group of men went down to the cellar to see if the woman might still be alive, but she was deceased. They did not touch her, left her where she lay, went back upstairs and closed the cellar door. Schnobrich noticed a potato masher lying on the frozen water with some dark stains on it. Officials were notified, and Dr. Alfred Muller performed the postmortem examination. Gertrude had contusions on the forehead, around the neck (consistent with strangulation), and a stab wound near the ribs on her left side. It appeared she had been raped either shortly before death or immediately afterward.

A warrant was issued for Andreas Schmidt and he was apprehended a short time later. At his preliminary hearing, Schmidt confessed to the crime and submitted a full, written confession in the German language, detailing how he killed Gertrude Roehl on January 26. The court ordered that Schmidt be held to answer to the crime of murder in the first degree, and his trial was scheduled for June 1867. However, he never stood trial because when Jailer, Gottlieb Scheef opened the cell door on June 17th, Schmidt was found dead, hanging by a rope made out of his pants and shirt—he had committed suicide. His trial was scheduled for the following morning, June 18th.

Andreas Schmidt was a German immigrant, between 40 and 50 years of age, of slender build, about 5'8" tall, with dark hair and full beard. He had a claim at Birch Coulee, Renville County, and had built a small shanty on the property, but had difficulty holding on to it. Schmidt had a hard time finding work and often thought of just burning his place down. The main reason he committed the brutal deed was that he had worked for Wilhelm Roehl for some time, had been abused, and cheated out of his pay, and wanted revenge. His first intention was to kill the man, but eventually came to the conclusion that if he killed him, it would be no punishment, as he wouldn't feel anything after death; but if he killed his family, he would grieve for years, and his revenge would be much greater. Schmidt was a desperate man struggling to survive. He suffered from depression and had attempted suicide by poisoning in the past. What if Roehl hadn't abused Schmidt and cheated him out of his pay—might this tragedy have been avoided? I guess we will never know for sure.

Redwood County was attached to Brown County for judicial purposes until 1872, the Schmidt case was the second murder case to be brought before the court, and became file #1 in the Redwood County judicial system.

The Pitchfork Murder

1888—Pitchfork used to beat John Rosenkranz, Willow Lake Township

This story begins when John Gorres, a respectable Willow Lake farmer, entered into a contract (for one year) with John Rosenkranz, a 25-year-old immigrant from Germany. Gorres had a wife and seven children, owned quite a bit of land and raised cattle and swine, so a hired hand was much needed on the farm. The two men worked together quite well, but there were times when a heated argument erupted. Gorres was known to have a raging temper, especially if he'd been drinking, when just about anything could set him off. But despite Gorres' frequent outbursts, the men managed to resolve their differences quickly and in a fair manner.

It was Monday, April 23, 1888, when Rosenkranz expressed dissatisfaction with his bargain; he asked for a settlement of his wages and said he would then leave the premises. Gorres consented, but asked the young man to stay and watch the children, while he and his wife went to town to get some money.

Upon their return, the children told their father that Rosenkranz, while packing his trunk, stowed away some hog rings and other small articles belonging to Gorres. When confronted by his employer, Rosenkranz did not deny it, but went upstairs with Gorres to retrieve the articles out of his trunk. Gorres scolded him for having taken the things in his absence, became very enraged and slapped Rosenkranz across the face. Feeling ashamed and angry, Rosenkranz went downstairs and out of the house. Gorres followed behind a few minutes later, yelling for Rosenkranz to come into the house to settle the matter and get his pay. But when he arrived downstairs, he found Rosenkranz standing at the door with a pitchfork, yelling, "I will kill you!" After quite a struggle over the pitchfork, Gorres got possession of it and struck Rosenkranz over the head with it, at least three times. Rosenkranz fell on his left side and holding his head up with his hand, cried, "Enough."

Gorres helped the beaten man upstairs and put him to bed, then went for a neighbor to have him check on Rosenkranz. He was found to be unconscious and a doctor was summoned. Shortly after Dr. Case arrived and assessed the situation, he knew there wasn't much he could do for the poor man. Rosenkranz was in very bad shape and had lost quite a bit of blood. He passed away around 9 p.m. His skull was not fractured, but there were three scalp wounds. Death was presumed to have been caused by concussion of the brain. Gorres surrendered himself to the local constable.

Gorres stated that he killed Rosenkranz in self-defense, but at the inquest, a spade with hairs and bloody spots on it had been found on the Gorres property. The prosecution's theory was that the blows were struck from behind, and so the body was exhumed, decapitated and the head brought into the courtroom and placed before the grand jury to be used as evidence to contradict Gorres' testimony. The grand jury found an indictment against Gorres for murder in the first degree. The trial was held in November and the jury determined that Gorres was not guilty as charged in the indictment, but was guilty of manslaughter in the first degree. He was sentenced to Stillwater State Prison for six years and six months, but on March 17, 1890, Gorres was pardoned by Governor William Merriam under the condition he abstain from liquor during the rest of his sentence. Gorres never touched another drop of liquor for the remainder of his life.

The Man who was Hung Twice

1888—Hangman's noose used to hang William Rose, Gales Township

This is the story of a bitter feud between the Lufkins and the Roses, which led to a murder that rivals anything to be found in the history of Redwood County. The Lufkin and Rose families came to Shetek Township, Murray County, around the same time in 1874, and settled in the same neighborhood. Moses Lufkin was a man who was universally despised and distrusted. He had family difficulties, and it was reported he separated from his wife before leaving Maine. He possessed a fair education and came from a good, old Maine family, but people claimed he was an eccentric old man, who lived with his two young daughters, Minnie and Grace.

On an adjoining farm on the opposite side of the road lived James Rose and his family. Rose and Lufkin had petty differences such as arise between neighbors. The trouble began when Rose and Lufkin had a dispute over a tree claim, and there were times when Lufkin's cow got into Rose's cornfield. From year-to-year the quarrels increased in bitterness until William Rose, James' eldest son, grew to manhood and sought to win the heart and hand of Grace Lufkin, but her father positively forbade William to court her. This added more fuel to the fire, and nothing but the destruction of Lufkin's family would appease William's mounting wrath.

It was a hot, moonlit night, on August 22, 1888, when members of the Slover family and Lufkin were engaged in casual conversation in the sitting room. There was a brightly lit kerosene lamp sitting on a table in the middle of the room. Eli sat near the east window where there was a cool breeze, while Lufkin sat on a comfortable lounge in front of the north window with his left shoulder and a portion of his back resting against the window casing. At about 8:15 p.m., a bullet came crashing through the window, whizzing through Lufkin's body and striking a stove in one corner of the room. All at once, Lufkin fell forward, grasped his chest, and exclaimed, "Help quick, I am shot through the body, deader than hay." Eli Slover then rushed to the window and thought he caught a glimpse of a man about twenty-five feet away fleeing the scene, but wasn't sure who it was.

Because of the ongoing feud, William Rose, became a likely suspect and was eventually arrested and convicted of murder in the first degree; purely on circumstantial evidence. Rose was acquitted at the first two trials, but at the third trial, Eli Slover, claimed he was now positive that it was William Rose he saw that night fleeing the scene. The jury brought in a guilty verdict and Judge Webber sentenced Rose to hang. The case was appealed; it went to the Supreme Court and eventually to the U.S. Supreme court, but the lower court's decision was upheld. Governor Merriam scheduled the execution for October 16, 1891.

It was a bungled execution. The first time the executioner pulled the lever, Rose dropped several feet, the rope was taut for a few moments and then broke, slamming Rose's body to the ground. He was unconscious, and carried back up to the platform. A second noose was placed around his neck, and the process was repeated. This time the rope held and the body dangled in the air for twenty-three minutes before the rope was severed and the body declared, "Dead".

William Rose and his death will be remembered, as these events brought home to the people of Minnesota the truth that executing criminals, was radically, morally, and terribly wrong. The State of Minnesota finally abolished capital punishment in 1911, making it one of twelve states, and the District of Columbia, where crimes are not punishable by death.

Death by Poisoning

*1896 -- Strychnine Poisoning, Charlie Shea commits suicide,
Hotel Francois, Redwood Falls*

Charlie Shea, twenty-one years of age, was night clerk and porter at Hotel Francois. He was a pleasant young man, and while behind the hotel counter, made friends for the hotel at all times. In the office, he never seemed despondent, but always seemed to look on the sunny side of life. It was when he was alone, occupying a chair in the office during the late night hours, that despondency would come over him and life's cloud would look the darkest. He had no enemies in the entire town; in fact, to know him was to like him. Despondency, induced by mental aberration, caused by strong drink, was undoubtedly the cause of his many depressed moods. Young Shea had threatened to take his life on several occasions, and when in these despondent moods, it was necessary to watch him closely.

Charlie Shea had purchased twenty-five grains of strychnine at Otto Schmahl's drug store in Redwood Falls sometime in November 1896. Clerk Palmer asked him what he wanted the poison for, and Shea immediately replied that he wanted it for killing rats. Shea registered his name and the purpose for using the drug so it could be sold to him.

At 6:00 a.m. on November 28, after the chef and other female employees of the hotel had gone into the kitchen, Shea went in and inquired if everything was all right. Receiving an affirmative reply he said, "Well, girls, I am going to make my last call of the commercial." He was gone about twenty minutes, and on returning, he pulled a small bottle from his pocket, seized a glass, and with a smile on his red face, he continued, "Well, girls, I won't be with you very long; I'll take my breakfast in hell." Then he poured nearly one-half of the contents of the one-eighth ounce of strychnine into a glass, poured some water on top of it, and with a single swallow, took all but two grains of the deadly drug. "There," he said, after performing this act, which did not even arouse the suspicions of the employees, "That will finish me in a short time. Maybe some of you girls want to join me. There is enough strychnine left in that bottle to end all of your lives."

Just as he was stepping out of the kitchen, and into the hall, the first spasm seized him. The convulsion was so strong that it stopped him in his tracks, and he stood dead still. Soon he inquired for some antidote. Then a second spasm came over him, stronger than the first. The employees called Clerk McCall and he summoned Dr. Flinn, and while they waited for the doctor, an attempt was made to force something down Shea's throat to kill the effects of the poison. Shea was carried into an adjoining room and placed on a bed. Dr. Flinn arrived a few minutes later and at once forced down Shea's throat several different liquids to destroy the effects of the poison. But the dose of strychnine was too large, and twenty minutes after Dr. Flinn arrived, Shea was dead.

The boarders at Hotel Francois, together with the employees, proprietor, and a number of the acquaintances of the deceased, after hearing from Shea's parents, decided to give the young man a religious burial. They purchased a lot in the Redwood Falls Cemetery for the last resting place of the remains, attended to all the funeral arrangements, but did not purchase a headstone. Rev. John Sinclair, who was acquainted with Charlie Shea, gave the funeral sermon. Swallowing strychnine must have been a very painful and excruciating way to die.

Hotel Francois, corner of Second & Washington Streets, Redwood Falls. Charlie Shea worked and died here, November 1896

17

Bludgeoned and Set on Fire

1897—Wagon King Pin used to bludgeon John O'Connel, and then set on fire, Westline Township

It happened on a hot, sultry evening July 31, 1897, at the farm site of John O'Connell, in Westline Township. Seven ugly gashes on his head, apparently made by some crude tool of iron were the direct cause of death. Three of the wounds fractured the skull in as many different places, and any one of the three wounds would have produced instant death. Two of the wounds, one on either side of the head, created fractures extending nearly to the top of the head. After this horrible deed had been committed, the murderer saturated his clothes with kerosene, and the building was set on fire. John's body was badly burned before he could be rescued from the flames.

On that fateful night, John O'Connell and a neighbor, Charles Gahaghan, returned from Amiret, Lyon County, about 8:00 p.m. Martha was quite upset with her husband and his friend, as both men appeared to be under the influence of alcohol, and John had brought a jug of whiskey home with him. Gahaghan left the O'Connell farm around 9:00 p.m. Their nine children retired around 9:30 p.m. or so and Martha went upstairs around 10:00 p.m. John, in a drunken stupor, prepared for bed an hour later. While he was with his wife, they indulged in a heated quarrel. Martha started down the stairs, and had reached the third or fourth step from the top. She wore her hair braided and hanging down behind her back. John reached over the railing and happened to catch his wife by the braided hair, drew her back to the second floor, and threw her down with great violence. This treatment produced the fit of insanity. She afterwards arose and went downstairs, and was soon followed by her husband. On passing down the steps, John took a seat on a trunk near the foot of the stairs, and the children claim to have heard him moan several times during the evening.

Sometime later, Martha gave a voluntary confession to attorney Clague. In this confession, she acknowledged having murdered her husband, but stated that she did it in self-defense. She said that John came home about 7:30 p.m., drunk with Charles Gahaghan. He brought home a jug of whisky with him, and drank frequently during the night. At about 10:00 p.m., she set the sponge for bread and shortly afterward retired. John came upstairs an hour later and peremptorily asked her to take the baby downstairs. She refused to do so, and on her refusal, he told her to get it out of the way or he would throw it out the window. More words passed between them and the husband struck the wife. Then she attempted to make her escape. Getting down the stairs a few steps, she was seized by the hair and dragged back by John, who threw her on the floor; her head and wrist being injured by the violent fall. Recovering, she again got up and this time made her escape followed by her husband, who was swearing and striking at her. She went outdoors and soon returned. On her return, John again came at her. She picked up a wagon king pin lying on the windowsill and came at him and continued to strike him with the pin until he fell over the trunk standing nearby. Further than this she knew nothing. When the two were upstairs, she pleaded with her husband not to make a row for the sake of her children.

The grand jury of Redwood County met at the November term of court in 1897; twenty-three members of the jury were present to return two indictments and reported that no bill had been found against Martha or her son, James. Judge Webber announced the fact and immediately ordered the release of Martha and James. The reason the grand jury refused to indict Martha was that it would be impossible to convict her; no twelve men on the jury would convict her, after hearing all of the evidence of the State. A future grand jury could have indicted Martha O'Connell, but this never happened. Martha continued with her life, raised her children, worked the farm, and lived to a ripe old age. She became well known in the area as the only woman who got away with murder.

A Cold Blooded Killing

1897—Pistol killed Fred Kuehn, Sherman Township

According to all the details of this horrible affair, the murder can be sized up as one of the most cold-blooded cases that ever occurred in the Southwestern section of Minnesota. It was premeditated with the procurement of a revolver and a single and a double-barreled pair of shotguns, without the slightest provocation known to civil annals. The revolver was pulled from the hip pocket of the murderer, and shots fired within just two feet of the victim.

The tragedy occurred on August 29, 1897, at the home of Fred Kuehn, a thirty-six year old farmer of considerable acreage residing in Sherman Township. He lived alone in a shanty by an isolated spot on the banks of the Wabasha River. Gustav Metag owned a large tract of land about one and a half miles from the house where the crime was committed. The previous spring a contract was entered into with Kuehn, whereby the latter was to farm his tract of one-hundred and twenty acres upon shares—but the question of threshing was a doubtful one in the contract. As the time approached for harvesting the crop, Metag wanted to thresh before doing the plowing. Kuehn objected and bad blood was created between the two.

On the day in question, Metag and his son went to Kuehn's to discuss the situation of threshing before doing any plowing. A heated exchange of hot words ensued; Kuehn insisting the plowing be done before threshing. Finally, Kuehn took his pipe out of his mouth and put it in his pocket. He then drew back the other hand as if to strike Metag. Then Metag placed his hand in his hip pocket, pulled a gun, and fired four shots rapidly. Kuehn fell back dead, and Metag jumped into his buggy and drove to Morgan, Redwood County, where he sought the village constable. After telling the story he was placed under arrest and was brought to Redwood Falls and lodged in the county jail.

Metag told officials that he always carried a gun when dealing with Kuehn, as he was a bad man and always wanted to fight. So he had a gun with him for his own protection. Kuehn's life had been littered with several actions, civil and otherwise, and had been the foundation for many complaints of crookedness—but there was nothing to aggravate the manner in which he was murdered.

Gustav Metag's trial began on May 3, 1898. He was charged with murder in the first degree. Defense Attorney Stuart stated that his side would introduce evidence to show that the act was justifiable. Metag testified on his own behalf, revealing numerous encounters where Kuehn had threatened his life with bodily harm. The jury deliberated for only three hours and returned the verdict, "Not guilty of the crime charged in the indictment, but guilty of murder in the second degree". Metag was sentenced to life in prison at Stillwater State Prison.

Many long years in a cold, dark cell went by before Metag filed an "Application for a commutation of his sentence" with the Board of Pardons upon the grounds "The ends of justice have been fully subserved." On January 28, 1914, the Board of Pardons, after hearing the case, commuted Metag's life sentence to thirty years. In April 1916, Gustav Metag made an application for discharge in order to be able to leave the state with his wife, who was in poor health, and take her to Colorado. The Metag case was presented at a regular meeting of the State Board of Parole held on December 15, 1916; the matter of final discharge of Gustav Metag was authorized and took effect that day. After his release from prison, Gustav Metag never had any more trouble with the law for the remainder of his life.

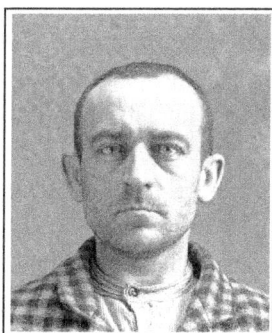

Gustav Metag
Served 18 yrs. of a life
sentence

Killed with an Iron Stake

1909—Heavy iron stake used to inflict blows to head, Cecil Norton,
Kintire Township

William Tibbetts was a seventy-year-old farmer living near Delhi, who was well thought of in the community. After his wife died young he was left to raise his four children on his own. For a time, he endeavored to keep house with the help of young daughter, Dorothy, who was about twelve years old. He then employed Rose Norton, a lady from St. Paul, to act as his housekeeper. Norton brought along her daughter, Cecil, who was eighteen years old at the time.

It was a Saturday in late August, 1909, when Rose Norton decided to take the two youngest Tibbetts children to Minneapolis, to shop and see the sites in the "big city." She expected to return on the midnight train Monday, and left her daughter, Cecil, to attend to the household chores.

On August 30, 1909, the family arose as usual and Dorothy and her older brother, Chauncey, went to the barn to attend to the chores. What transpired in the house will probably never be known, but Cecil Norton was killed by blows to her temple and head with a heavy iron stake used to gouge out caked salt from the barrel. The force from the blows crushed her skull so that her brains protruded from the wounds. Then Tibbetts went to the barn and collected a pile of hay. He brought it into the house, piled it over Cecil's body, and set it on fire. Chauncey upon seeing the smoke ran to David McNaughton's house, about half a mile away, and told him about the fire. McNaughton notified the town of Delhi and several neighbors who rushed to the Tibbetts house.

When Chauncey left the Tibbetts farm, little Dorothy was still in the barn. It was thought that she saw the fire and rushed to the house. Dorothy saw enough to alarm her and started to run, when her father struck her down with a murderous blow to the back of her head. She fell in a pool of blood in her father's bedroom near the hallway, connecting this room with the stairway and kitchen. Then her father brought in more hay, piled it over her body, and also set this on fire.

The neighbors began dousing the fire with many pails of water. Roy Leonard heard a groan under the blazing hay in the bedroom and kicking it apart, brought out little Dorothy, who was still breathing but unconscious. She was carried out of the blaze but died almost immediately. Chauncey told the men who carried her out that it was not Dorothy, as she was in the barn, but upon seeing his sister, he became hysterical with fright and grief and was taken to Mr. Berg's place. This discovery at once drew the attention of the men to another blazing pile in the parlor, and the charred and mutilated body of Cecil Norton was discovered.

In the excitement of these gruesome findings of foul murder, Tibbetts was lost sight of, but as soon as the fire was extinguished a search was made. His body was found dangling from a halter strap's end in the same scuttle hole where he had thrown down the hay to conceal his crimes.

The jury rendered their verdict that the two girls came to their death from blows inflicted by William Tibbetts and that he came to his death by strangulation by his own hands.

Rose Norton arrived from St. Paul Park overwhelmed with grief over the tragedy, and the next day took the remains of her only daughter back for burial. A short service was held at the town hall in Delhi over the remains of little Dorothy and her father, after which they were given burial in the Redwood Falls Cemetery. There was also a special memorial service held at the Presbyterian Church in Delhi, in honor of little Dorothy, whose death, at the hands of her own father seemed inscrutably hard to comprehend.

What happened in the early morning hours of August 30, 1909, one can only imagine. Neighbors thought Tibbetts to be quite "queer." No motive was assigned for the double murder and suicide. People claimed the man had been unbalanced mentally for quite some time.

William and Dorothy Tibbetts gravestones, Redwood Falls Cemetery (photos by author)

The Worst Arson in Redwood

1915—Arson destroys Drews Hotel, Seaforth, Sheridan Township

Redwood County's biggest case of arson took place in Seaforth. The story goes that two Sanborn real estate men, T.H. Jordan and M.E. Garvey, bought the former Gustav Drews Hotel in Sheridan Township on February 1, 1915, from Alvin Longbottom, trading him North Dakota farmland for it. They insured the hotel for $3,000, and then on March 20, the partners dealt with J.W. Keyes, drawing up papers in the Seaforth Bank showing that Keyes had paid $1,000 and promised to pay $1,000 annually until the $10,000 purchase was met.

Sometime around midnight April 4, 1915 (Easter Sunday) it was discovered that the Drews Hotel was on fire. Frank Smetak, one of the hotel residents, smelled smoke and was one of the first people in the building to awaken. With lantern in hand, he hurried down the halls shouting to people to get out of their beds. The hotel burned to the ground.

People were suspicious and soon Keyes, Jordan, and Garvey were under arrest, charged with first-degree arson. In the early part of May, Mr. Keyes made a confession that he set fire to the hotel. Keyes stated that he did the deed through a scheme put up by T.H. Jordan of Benson and M.E. Garvey of Graceville. Jordan and Garvey were held in the Redwood County Jail, awaiting the preliminary hearing held at Lamberton before Justice L.A. Gooler. Attorney A.H. Enersen had charge of the prosecution for the State. Jordan and Garvey stated they knew nothing about the burning of the hotel.

During Keyes' trial, he confessed to setting fire to the hotel building at a time when he knew it was occupied by human beings. In his confession, he implicated Jordan and Garvey, asserting that it was at their instigation the building was burned in order that the insurance money might be obtained. Keyes pleaded guilty to the charge of first-degree arson and was sentenced to ten years in the Stillwater State Prison.

In April 1916, T.H. Jordan was being tried a second time for first-degree arson. Jordan was defended by Attorneys Frank Murphy of Wheaton and Frank Clague of Redwood Falls. Very little new evidence was brought into the case. At the time of Jordan's first trial in November 1915, the jury disagreed after thirty hours of deliberation, but at Jordan's second trial, he was found guilty of first-degree arson after only several hours' deliberation by the jury. Judge Olsen sentenced Jordan to the Stillwater State Prison for ten years.

In November 1916, Garvey's case finally came up for trial. After Jordan's case was closed, Jordan turned State's evidence and admitted that he had hired Keyes to do the burning and also implicated Garvey in the deal, but it appeared that aside from the stories told by Jordan and Keyes, there was not enough evidence to convict Garvey. The trial lasted only a few days, and after only four hours of deliberation, the jury brought in a verdict of "not guilty." But Garvey's legal matters didn't end there. He was indicted by the grand jury in April 1917 for committing perjury at his trial the previous November.

Garvey was in court for a third trial, on a charge of perjury, in the district court in November 1917. He was implicated and was finally proven not guilty of cooperating with Jordan and Keyes in the Seaforth arson case. The jury brought in a verdict of "not guilty" after being out for only twenty minutes. Garvey left that same day for his home in Graceville. This finally closed all the cases which grew out of the burning of the Drew's Hotel and which held the attention of the court for so many years.

Drew Hotel in Seaforth (Courtesy Redwood County Hist. Soc.)

Drew Hotel after the fire, April 1915
(Courtesy Redwood County Hist. Soc.)

Ax Murders and Suicide

1917—Ax kills Kleeman family and a suicide, Clements.

William Kleeman, a young farmer, with a wife and four small children lived near Clements for about two years. The couple had been married eight years and both were from prominent families in the area. To help with household expenses, they took in a teacher, Ruth Snyder, as a boarder and the arrangement seemed to work out quite well. Ruth helped out with the children and other household chores when needed.

On Friday, March 23, 1917, William Kleeman drove Snyder to town so she could take the train to Mankato to visit her parents over the weekend. On that day, William complained of not feeling well, and asked her to take a livery on her return trip so he would not have to come to town for her. Ruth kindly obliged with the agreement as she noticed Kleeman's odd behavior during the past few weeks.

When Snyder returned on Sunday evening, the liveryman, who drove her out from Morgan was unable to get to the Kleeman place because the roads were so muddy. Ruth Snyder exited the buggy and walked in the mud nearly half a mile before she reached her destination. Upon approaching the house, she found everything quite still, and trying the door, found it unlocked. She wondered at the silence of the place as she entered the kitchen in the gathering darkness. She lit a match and then stopped short, as William Kleeman's body confronted her—hanging from a rope attached to a hook in the ceiling. He was partially dressed, having on his shirt and trousers, but no shoes or socks. A chair on which he had stood had been pushed away after he had adjusted the rope around his neck. With unusual coolness and courage, she seized a butcher knife from the table, mounted the same chair used by Kleeman, cut the rope and stumbled to the floor as the body pulled her down. For some time, she strove to revive the man, but it was too late. He was already dead. The door to the bedroom adjoining the kitchen was open, and in the faint light, she saw an ax caked with blood lying on the floor. Mrs. Kleeman and the six-week-old baby, Eileen, were dead in bed in one room and the three

Kleeman gravestones, Redwood Falls Cemetery (photos by author)

other children in another room. It appeared that the killing had been done either late Saturday night, or early Sunday morning, while Mrs. Kleeman and the children were asleep.

The only message Kleeman left to explain his deeds was a poorly written note, of which the meaning is hardly intelligible—"Dear Folks, when I woke this morning someone in the house said, 'Money or Life,' It is it dresses. Happy. I hang myself. Good-bye, bye. With love, W.E. Kleeman." Upon the side of the note was written, as a kind of afterthought: "He killed them."

The funeral of Mr. Kleeman and the two oldest children was held at the Methodist Church, Rev. Darrell preaching the sermon, and internment was at the Redwood Falls Cemetery. The funeral of Mrs. Kleeman and her two smallest babies was held at Church of the Holy Communion; Dr. A.A. Joss gave the service and Rev. Darrell gave a short service at the burial site—internment was in the local cemetery. Mrs. Kleeman was the only daughter of Mr. and Mrs. Henry Petrie of Paxton Township. The four children were Gladys, aged five; Lois, four; Jordon, two; and Eileen, a baby of about six weeks. Neighbors reported the family had been heavily in debt, causing William to constantly brood over his debts and his inability to pay them, resulting in a fit of insanity. However, relatives stated the family had no cause for anxiety over money matters. It was thought that the horrible deed was the act of a deranged mind, although the exact particulars will never be known. It was certainly a sad thing to see a family of that size blotted out of existence in such a tragic manner.

Ruth Snyder resigned her position as teacher, and returned to her home in Mankato, stating that she would never return to this part of the country again.

Shotgun Murder

1921—Shotgun kills Leslie Joslin, Honner Township

Hall Green, a 26 year-old black, Paxton Township farm-hand, was given a life sentence for the shotgun slaying on April 8, 1921, of Leslie Joslin, whose body was discovered near a road two miles east of Redwood Falls the following morning. Never were details of a modern crime skimpier. Court records reveal none of the testimony and newspaper accounts handled the subject as if it were too sordid to touch. The *Redwood Gazette* labeled the motive "jealousy", stating only that the murder occurred when Joslin, whose parents lived in Morton, was returning to the home of an uncle with whom he lived, after spending the evening with the neighbor's daughter, Mabel Humphrey, who was seventeen years old.

A sidelight of the trial was the arrest of Green's brother, Henry, "on evidence brought out in the trial." Henry was subsequently convicted of the rape of Mabel Humphrey, and joined Hall in the penitentiary. Henry was sentenced from one to seven years at Stillwater State Prison. Hall was sentenced to life imprisonment, but was granted an unconditional release May 16, 1960, after having served thirty-nine years of his sentence.

It would appear that Hall Green, a man of color, did not receive a fair trial in 1921. Sheriff Kise and Attorney Dolliff never located witnesses to corroborate Hall's whereabouts in Redwood Falls on the night of the murder, or locate the unidentified white man who was seen by witnesses in the vicinity of the crime that night. And County Attorney A.H. Enersen stated, "Sheriff Kise did very excellent work and his loyal help at every move made by the State added greatly to the facility with which the case was disposed of...and I feel confidently that we have the right party; while much of the evidence is circumstantial, yet it fitted in so nicely on the only reasonable theory—that being the guilt of the defendant—that we could not get away from the force of it."

One of the jurors, Gust Wurscher, stated that he felt the evidence presented at the trial, and the failure of Hall Green to establish an alibi, satisfied the jury, and rendered him the guilty party. Hall maintained his innocence throughout the trial—felt he'd been framed, and was quite certain that Attorney Dolliff was protecting the real murderer. Hall stated that bootleggers were responsible for Joslin's death, but this claim was never investigated further.

It's quite evident that our justice system in the 1920s failed in presenting a proper defense for Hall Green. In this case, the crime was committed on April 8, the trial started on April 27, Green was sentenced on April 30, and transported to prison on May 3—less than thirty days, quite an unusual circumstance in a case of first-degree murder.

Hall Green, age 26, May 1921
(Courtesy MN Historical Society

Paranormal Investigating

Equipment and artifacts

A collective organization of scholars and scientists for the exploration and study of paranormal activity was founded in London in 1882, it was called *The Society for Psychical Research*. This society represented one of the first attempts at correlating and evaluating information collected on paranormal phenomena. This enthusiasm for finding answers about the afterlife continued into the twentieth century with investigators like British psychic researcher Henry Price (1881-1948). This created a great public interest in his work, especially the 1937-38 investigation of the now infamously haunted Borley Rectory in Essex, England.

The techniques and methodologies Henry Price employed during this era have not changed greatly. So it could be argued that the only way paranormal investigating has moved forward in the last one hundred and thirty years is through the introduction of new technology—with the earliest recordings captured on magnetic tape now replaced with digital voice recorders.

Military scientific advancements have now disseminated down to the general public, allowing the paranormal and UFO investigator to access affordable thermal imaging cameras and infrared technology. It is now commonplace to have easily accessible digital photography, audio recording technology, video and thermal imaging recordings, apps and tools—all designed to aid in the process of connecting us with the other side.

Equipment

Digital Voice Recorders (DVRs) are used by the paranormal investigator to document the vigils and ghost box sessions. It has been my experience that when listening to disembodied voices only a small percentage of the conversation is heard in real time, with the majority being documented via the recording. It is believed that some dialogues are only picked-up on these devices because they are capable of recording at wider frequency to that of our own hearing. DVRs are also used to record Electronic Voice Phenomena (EVPs). This is when you are able to hear a voice without any other equipment being used—as if the spirit is standing next to you and whispering in your ear. I use both very advanced DVRs that have twin tubular condensing microphones as well as the cheaper models—as these devices do not have options to filter out what we would consider to be the background noise and rubbish in order to pick up only what I am seeking to record.

The display highlights the evolution of recording audio evidence on paranormal investigations, from the first heavy portable magnetic tape twin reel recording equipment of the early 1960s, to the tape cassette recorder and Dictaphone devices of the 1970s and 80s, through to the first Sony digital recorders of the late 1990s, and the most modern Olympus digital twin condensing mics.

Infrared laser thermometers infers temperature from a portion of the thermal radiation sometimes called blackbody radiation emitted by the object being measured. The laser is used to help aim the thermometer allowing for the temperature to be measured from a distance. By knowing the amount of infrared energy emitted by the object and its emissivity, the object's temperature can often be determined. Infrared thermometers are a subset of devices known as "thermal radiation thermometers".

It is a useful tool when checking any dramatic changes in the temperature of trigger object—when they are interacted with, and for when team members feel they are being touched. This very device was mention in the Soap Factory and Chase on the Lake chapters of *Mysterious Minnesota*—when I saw shadow figures breaking the beam.

Cameras have been used to create and capture paranormal activity from the first moment they were invented. Victorian photographers took great delight in superimposing images to create creepy tableaus, where a husband and wife would be seen with the husband holding his wife's decapitated head in his hands. Ghosts were placed into images by photography darkroom techniques, and placed into plate photographs to create awe and wonder.

A famous example of this would be the *Cottingley Fairies* that appeared in a series of five photographs taken by Elsie Wright (1901–88) and Frances Griffiths (1907–86), two young cousins who lived in Cottingley, near Bradford in England. In 1917, when the first two photographs were taken, Elsie was sixteen years old and Frances was nine. The pictures came to the attention of writer Sir Arthur Conan Doyle, who used them to illustrate an article on fairies he had been commissioned to write for the Christmas 1920 edition of *The Strand Magazine*. Doyle, as a spiritualist, was enthusiastic about the photographs, and interpreted them as clear and visible evidence of psychic phenomena. Public reaction was mixed; some accepted the images as genuine, but others believed they had been faked.

The display highlights the way paranormal investigators could embrace photography as soon as cameras became portable, and moved away from the large heavy wooden boxes with glass and brass lenses set on a tripod, with a five minute exposure time. The box Brownie camera was at the forefront of this portability. The Brownie camera, introduced in 1900, invented low-cost photography by developing the concept of the snapshot to the masses.

The advent of the Single Lens Reflex (SLR) camera in the 1960s became the preferred design for paranormal investigators, but it was necessary to inform the pharmacist that the smoky and blurred images they developed during the processing were actually wanted, and not to be placed in the trash. The introduction of digital point-and-shoot cameras in 1990s, through the 2010s with LCD viewfinder displays, reduced the appeal of the SLR. It is now possible to take sharp and professional photographs on cellphones, with options for infrared and thermal imaging, complete with filters.

Full spectrum cameras are now also cheaply and widely available that take photographs in a full electromagnetic spectrum, from infrared to ultraviolet. This is a useful tool when you can see more through the viewing screen than you can with your own eyes.

Electrical Magnetic Field (EMF) Meters are used to measure the amount of ambient electrical magnetic energy in a location. It is believed that ghosts need energy to be able to manifest and be physical. This is said to be EMF energy and can be measured. A *K2* EMF meter is a handheld device that registers electrical energy in a series of colored LEDs—EMF is measured in a unit of energy called a gauss.

The Melmeter (on display) is a tool that also measures EMF, but has a calibrated and more accurate numbered digital display. It is possible to have a very basic dialogue with a spirit using these devices if the entity moves back-and-forth over the device to register a reading in response to a question asked. Fuse boxes, electrical sockets, and electric poles will register an EMF reading.

The Melmeter, digital voice recorders. and laser thermometer have all been used on paranormal investigations undertaken in the Redwood County museum, the Redwood Falls courthouse, the Francois Hotel building, the Redwood Theater, Birch Coulee Battlefield, Morton School, the Renville County Museum and grounds, Bechyn parsonage, church and cemetery, Danube Railway Museum, and the Renville County courthouse in Olivia. As well as the following locations across the Midwest and all over the world:

Minneapolis City Hall, Minnesota; Palmer House Hotel, Sauk Centre, Minnesota; The Mounds Theater, St. Paul, Minnesota; Wabasha Street Caves, St. Paul, Minnesota; The Soap Factory, Minneapolis, Minnesota; Fort Snelling, St. Paul, Minnesota; The Schmidt Brewery, St. Paul, Minnesota; The LeDuc Estate, Hastings, Minnesota; The Opera House, Mantorville, Minnesota; S.S. William Irvin, Duluth, Minnesota; Old Jail House bed and breakfast, Taylors Falls, Minnesota; Sweets Hotel, LeRoy, Minnesota; The Corner Drugstore, Sauk Centre, Minnesota; The Chase Resort Hotel, Walker, Minnesota; The St. James Hotel, Red Wing, Minnesota; The Boggs House, Mantorville, Minnesota; The Christie House, Long Prairie, Minnesota; The First National Bank, Long Prairie, Minnesota; The Kemp Block Opera House, Long Prairie, Minnesota; Loon Lake Cemetery, Jackson, Minnesota; The Pioneer Village, Jackson, Minnesota; The Rathbun Dugout, Jackson, Minnesota; Windom Area

Central School, Windom, Minnesota; The State Theater, Windom, Minnesota; Windom Public Library, Windom, Minnesota; The Bradshaw House Hotel, Baldwin, Wisconsin; The Wieting Opera House, Toledo, Iowa; The Railroad Crossing, Sanborn, Minnesota; Forepaugh's Restaurant, St. Paul, Minnesota; The Lund-Hoel House, Canby, Minnesota; The Canby Theater, Canby, Minnesota; The Pioneer Memorial, Sioux Falls, South Dakota; The S.S. Meteor, Superior, Wisconsin; Fairlawn Mansion, Superior, Wisconsin; The Masonic Temple, Superior, Wisconsin; Split Rock Lighthouse, Twin Harbors, Minnesota; The Maxfield House, Mankato, Minnesota; Pipestone County Museum, Pipestone, Minnesota; The Periwinkle Hotel, Chelsea, Iowa; Redwood County Museum, Redwood Falls, Minnesota; Renville County Historical Society, Morton, Minnesota; Morton High School, Morton, Minnesota; Fire Station Museum, Superior, Wisconsin; Queen Mary, Long Beach, California; Pendergast/Fish Building, Sauk Center, Minnesota; Peterborough Museum, Cambridgeshire, England; Boxmoor Common, Hertforshire, England; Tilbury Fort, Essex, England; The London Dungeons, Tooley Street, London, England; The Old Sessions House, Clerkenwell, London, England; Moot Hall, Maldon, England; Eastbury Manor, Barking, London, England; Houghton House, Bedfordshire, England; Old School House, Derby, England; Chislehurst Caves, Kent, England; Elizabethan House, Braintree, Essex; Tommy Knockers Pond, Bedfordshire, England; Rollright Stones, Oxfordshire, England; Stanton Low, Milton Keynes, England; The Knife and Cleaver pub, Bedfordshire, England; Nasby Battlefield, Northamptonshire, England; Bovingdon Airfield, Hertfordshire, England; Broxbourne Wood, England; Letchworth Museum, Hertfordshire, England; The Swan, Ampthill, England.

Haunted Dolls

Emma and Elsie

I received a phone call from an antiques shop in Alexandria, Minnesota. They were concerned that a Victorian doll in their possession kept being brought back to the shop, after it had been sold. On each occasion the new owners of the doll would bring it back a few days later after complaining of ghostly activity starting in their houses. This involved the lights and televisions turning themselves on-and-off on their own. I collected the doll and named her Emma (Little Ems). From the first moment I held her I could feel the energy, as if she was full of wasps. That night in my own house the television turned itself on in the early hours of the morning.

After blessing the doll and working with her over a period of time, she has been embrace by The International Paranormal Society and taken to many paranormal locations to use as a trigger object for spirit children—including the St. James Hotel in Red Wing, the Chase on the Lake Resort in Walker, the Historical Society of Melrose, and the Corner Drug Store in Sauk Centre. Emma is pictured on the back of this guide.

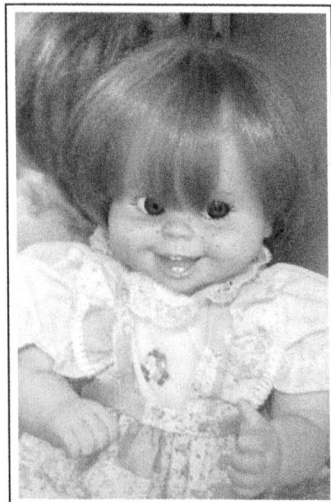

Elsie from Long Prairie

I went to investigate an antiques shop in Long Prairie, in Todd County. They had complained of paranormal activity, including the sighting of full-bodied apparitions and the hearing of voices. I tracked the majority of the activity down to a doll they had in their shop I have called Elsie. When I ran a K2 EMF meter over her she produced a very high spike of EMF at twenty-five Milligauss. When I took the doll away the paranormal activity ceased.

Books

Hans Holzer (1920–2009) was an American paranormal researcher and author. He wrote more than one-hundred and twenty books on supernatural and occult subjects, as well as several plays, musicals, films, and documentaries.

Holzer's most famous investigation was into the Amityville house case at 112 Ocean Avenue, Amityville, New York, in January 1977. Holzer and spiritual medium Ethel Meyers both investigated the property, with Meyers claiming that the house was built over an ancient Native American burial ground. She believed an angry spirit of a <u>Shinnecock</u> Indian Chief had possessed the previous occupant, driving him to murder his family. Photographs taken at the scene revealed several curious anomalies, such as the halos that appeared in the supposed images of bullet marks made in the original 1974 murders.

William Peter Blatty (1928-2017) was an American writer and filmmaker best known for his 1971 novel *The Exorcist*, and for the Academy Award-winning winning screenplay of its film adaptation. The book details the demonic possession of a twelve-year-old daughter of a famous actress, and the two priests who attempt to exorcise the demon. The novel was inspired by a 1949 case of demonic possession and exorcism that Blatty heard about while he was a student. Father Walter H. Halloran (1921-2005) was born and raised in Jackson, Minnesota, and was the Jesuit Priest who assisted in the original exorcism.

The St. Mary Medallions

The most elegant and luxurious room in the St. James Hotel in Red Wing, Minnesota, is room 210. It is trimmed in rich walnut with dark red textiles and leather paneled walls, produced from the Red Wing's own tannery. It also boasts fourteen foot high ceilings and a breathtaking view of Barn Bluff. This was the room originally used as the boardroom for meetings held by the Red Wing Shoe Company.

On one investigation Heather (team leader and EVP expert with The International Paranormal Society) went into the Boardroom suite to undertake a baseline test and to prepare the room for a vigil. She placed her iPad on the four-poster bed and conducted her tests. When she went to retrieve her iPad she noticed a small silver St. Mary medallion had suddenly appeared inside the case. This pendant was without the chain and had manifested out of thin air.

Heather came back down to the control area we had set up in the dining room and described what had happened—she showed the team the medallion with the religious iconography of Mary embossed onto it. I went directly back to the room after hearing of this phenomena to psychically see if any spirits or energies were still present. As I stepped into the room I instantly saw a glinting silver object laying in the middle of the red patterned Victorian designed carpet. Astoundingly, it was second silver St. Mary medallion—this new object was not present when Heather had been in the room just five minutes earlier. Once again it was without a chain, but with a slightly different design to the first pendant.

It is common for spirits to hide and move objects, as experienced with my watch and witnessed in the Wabasha Street Caves. I don't believe spirits can take physical objects with them to-and-from the spirit realm, but it would be possible for spirits to squirrel items away to use and present at a later date. I believe that a spirit stole two St. Mary medallions from the guests over a period of time—and then stored them somewhere away from prying eyes. Whether as a visual statement, or as a form of communication, the spirit then choose to reveal them to the team at this time.

Post-Mortem Photography

Post-mortem photography (also known as memorial portraiture or a mourning portrait) is the practice of photographing the recently deceased. These photographs of deceased loved ones were a normal part of American and European culture in the nineteenth and early twentieth centuries. Commissioned by grieving families, postmortem photographs not only helped in grieving, but often represented the only visual remembrance of the deceased and were among a family's most precious possessions. The long exposure time made deceased subjects easy to photograph. Clients would prefer to capture an image of a deceased loved one, rather than have no photograph at all.

These photographs served as keepsakes to remember the deceased. This was especially common with infants and young children. Victorian era childhood mortality rates were extremely high, and a post-mortem photograph might have been the only image of the child the family ever had. The later invention of the *carte de visite*, allowed multiple prints to be made from a single negative, meaning that copies of the image could be mailed to relatives.

The practice eventually peaked in popularity around the end of the 19th century and died out as "snapshot" photography became more commonplace. On display is the original photograph of a deceased infant that came from New London, Minnesota.

Ouija Boards

The Ouija board as we know it, with its distinctive alphabet design and separate planchette, was not patented until 1890—but letters drawn on a table or a plate were used with a pendulum before this. The interest in spiritualism was thriving throughout the Midwest during this period, and many lectures and séances took place as traveling spiritualists would come into towns like Redwood Falls to perform. One such performer was recorded in the Sauk Centre House, Sauk Centre, Minnesota. This is shown during the week of August 9, 1872, when five séances were practiced by J. L. Potter and H. H. Smith:

Spiritualism—Messrs. J. L. Potter and H. H. Smith, who lectured here last fall, are coming again and will give four or five lectures, commencing August 9th.

The following year Mr. Potter was back, and he once again performed his skills in front of an enthusiastic Sauk Centre audience:

December 6, 1873: Spiritualism—J. L. Potter, trance speaker, who travels under the auspices of a State Society or organization of Spiritualists lectured here five evenings ending on Sunday last. Our Citizens manifested their usual liberality and willingness to hear new theories and doctrines by a large attendance.

General William LeDuc of the LeDuc Estate in Hastings, Minnesota, was intrigued by spiritualism and held regular séances in the parlor and dining room of his home. Spiritualism developed throughout the latter half of the nineteenth century and reached its peak by the early twentieth century. It was said to have over eight million participants throughout the United States and Europe. Many followers, like William, were drawn from the middle and upper classes. The rapping sounds, the playing of musical instruments, automatic writing, and divination appeared to present tangible evidence that practical-minded Americans found difficult to ignore.

It is believed William LeDuc used such a *talking board* during his séance sessions. It is possible that he opened up a window or a portal during his séances through which any number of spirits could have traveled without discrimination. It is therefore possible that the reported hauntings of the LeDuc house have no relation to the family, or have no connection with the area or house.

Ouija boards are now available in the children's toy aisle at Wal-Mart. The ones on display have been given to Adrian Lee for protection as they have been used, or purchased from thrift shops to stop people and children from using them.

Voodoo and Hoodoo

Louisiana Voodoo, also known as New Orleans Voodoo, describes a set of spiritual folkways developed from the traditions of the African diaspora. It is a cultural form of the Afro-American religions developed by enslaved West and Central Africans populations of the US state of Louisiana. Voodoo became syncretized with the catholic and Francophile culture of New Orleans as a result of the African cultural oppression in the region resulting from the Atlantic slave trade. It was through Louisiana Voodoo that terms such as *Voodoo dolls* were introduced into the American lexicon. The Voodoo powder on display is from New Orleans and is used as incense for clearing a space of negative energies and entities.

Alligators, caimans, and crocodiles have also long been used in southern conjure. We can trace the roots of this practice to the veneration of crocodiles in Africa when we pay attention to Southern folklore. The alligator is an animal of great significance to both Native Americans and traditional African cultures. Various parts of the alligator are deemed to carry special medicine, including the head, feet, claws and teeth.

Alligator heads are also used by believers in Juju type charms. A small alligator head can be set on a shelf near the front door, with its mouth open as a protection for the household, drawing on its protective territorial nature. This can often be seen throughout the South, particularly in Florida and Louisiana. Some believe the spirit of the alligator resides in the head itself. In this context, the head is called a *gad*. You can also place a gator head over a prosperity bowl so it can protect your money.

Kuman Thong

Kuman Thong is a household divinity of Thai popular religion. It is believed to bring luck and fortune to the owner if properly revered— *Kuman* means *Sanctified young boy* and *thong* means golden. The veneration of Kuman Thong is not part of mainstream Buddhist practices, but has been popular in Thailand since ancient times.

The authentic Kuman Thong originated in a practice of necromancy. They were obtained from the desiccated fetuses of children who had died whilst still in their mothers' womb. The witch doctors were said to have the power to invoke these stillborn babies, adopt them as their children, and use them to help them in their endeavors. This would also allow the spirit to live a long life after their physical life had been cut short in-utero or as a small infant.

The Kuman Thong on display is an original ceramic effigy from Thailand, he is wrapped in a Buddhist spell with dirt from a graveyard. In Buddhist culture he will bring good luck and has offerings of candy.

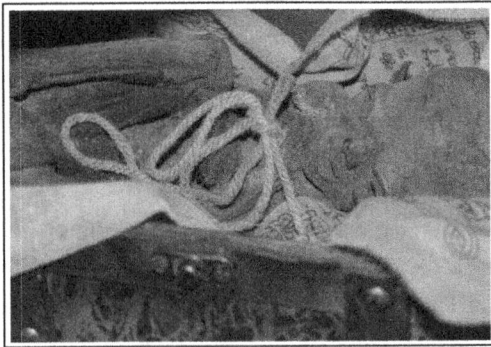

Kuman Thong from Thailand

Vampire Protection for Travelers

The notion of vampirism has existed for millennia. Cultures such as the Mesopotamians, Hebrews, Ancient Greeks, and Romans had tales of demons and spirits which are considered precursors to modern vampires. However, despite the occurrence of vampire-like creatures in these ancient civilizations, the folklore for the entity we know today as the vampire originates almost exclusively from early-18th-century southeastern Europe. When verbal traditions of many ethnic groups of the region were recorded and published. In most cases, vampires are revenants of evil beings, suicide victims, or witches, but they can also be created by a malevolent spirit possessing a corpse or by being bitten by a vampire. Belief in such legends became so pervasive that in some areas it caused mass hysteria and even public executions of people believed to be vampires.

When immigrants came to Minnesota from Bohemia, Germany and the Eastern European countries, it was common for travelers to protect themselves from the perceived threat of vampires—especially in an unknown land. These kits and cases contained everything a worried traveler would need to disarm or protect against a vampire attack. This would include a Bible, Crucifix, rosary, holy water, garlic, salt, mallet, pliers or pincers (for the removing teeth) and sometimes even the stake itself—although they could easily be manufactured at each location with a branch and a sharp knife. The artifacts in the vampire protection kits are authentic—the boxes are reproductions.

Spirit Dolls

Spirit dolls are used across the globe in many cultures. The Asian dolls on display have been blessed by a Buddhist monk. After purchasing a doll the owner brings it to a monk who conducts a prayer and an anointing ceremony known as *plook sek*. Such prayers are normally used to bless lucky amulets, which are also popular in Asian culture, where ancient beliefs in magic are still prevalent. In the case of *luk thep*, it is often seen as a way of animating the doll, where a wandering spirit is invited to inhabit it and give it a soul.

In Guatemalan tradition worry dolls are given or lent to brooding and sorrowful children. They would tell their doll about their sorrows, fears and worries, then hide it under their pillow during the night. After this, the child will literally sleep over the whole thing. At the next morning, all sorrows are said to have been taken away by the worry doll. This tradition came from a local legend about the origin of the *Muñeca quitapena* and refers to a Mayan princess named *Ixmucane*. The princess received a special gift from the sun god which would allow her to solve any problem a human could worry about.

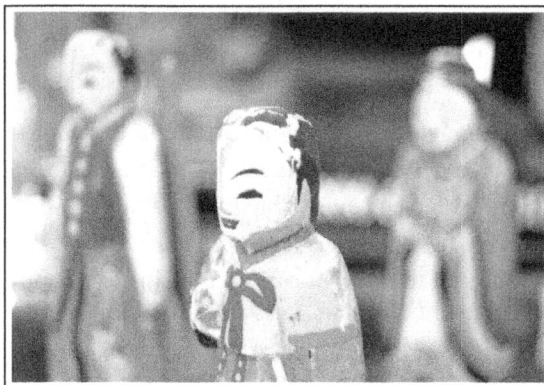

Asian Spirit People

Spell

A spell, charm, invocation, or hex is a set of words, spoken or unspoken, which are considered by its user to invoke some magical effect. Historical attestations exist for the use of some variety of incantations in many cultures around the world. Spells can be used in calling upon or summoning a spirit, demon, god, or other supernatural agent (evocation), or to prevent a person from taking some action or in forcing them to remain on some path of action (*binding spells*). The spell on display is for hair regrowth, and was cast by a witch as part of a coven in Sauk Centre, Minnesota, in 2009.

Photographs

Before every investigation we take hundreds of photographs of each room at the location. This procedure comes as part of our baseline tests and acts as the perfect way to document the environments we will be working in. These photographs become an important tool for reference if an object moves during a vigil or a door slams in another part of the house. We can then look back to see how the objects were placed before the paranormal activity occurred. It also acts as a useful *aid memoir* when describing the locations I investigate.

Heather completed this task during the Christie House investigation in Long Prairie, Minnesota. In the attic she moved around the space photographing and documenting every aspect of the interior, from the furniture to the decorative objects. She took several photographs of a small dresser with drawers and a rectangular wooden-framed mirror. A pencil portrait of Ida Christie's daughter Lucille was resting against the mirror.

After the investigation Heather uploaded the photographs she had taken of the attic. In the picture she had taken of the coat and dresser she saw the face of a man looking back at her in the sliver of mirror between the gold-gilded picture frame and the wooden surround. This was a chilling experience for Heather when she realized that the ghost she had captured as a reflection must have been standing next to her without her knowledge. The man's face was flesh colored and looked very real and three-dimensional. He had the look of a more elderly gentleman with slightly drawn eyes and a balding head. None of the men investigating this property on my team remotely fit this description and Heather was working by herself when she took the photographs. This is a remarkable piece of evidence and to capture the face of an apparition is exceptionally rare. We then looked to ascertain who this ghostly face might belong to. Lorna said he looked exactly like Dr. George Christie, so we compared the image of the ghostly face to a portrait of Dr. Christie hanging in the study. The resemblance was remarkable and based on the visual evidence presented here I am confident in saying that the ghostly image in the mirror is that of Dr. George Christie who died in 1947. He appears to still be residing in the house he once built and loved.

On the left is the photograph of the ghostly face reflected in the mirror—just above the frame of the portrait

Above are two portraits of Doctor George Christie for comparison, taken at different times of his life. Note the same receding hairline, the shape of the face, the dark eyebrows, prominent nose, and downturn of the mouth

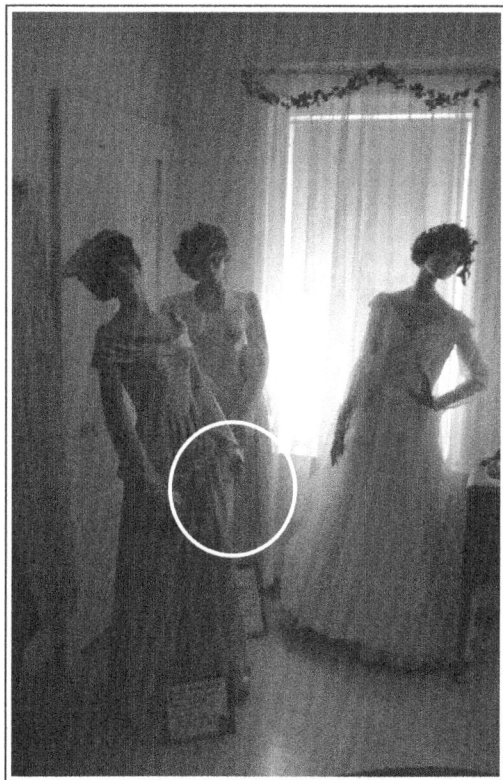

On the left is a photograph taken in the wedding room of the Redwood Falls Historical Society Museum during the baseline photographs before an investigation. Passing through the mannequin's hand is a beam of light blue energy that was not present on the other five photographs that were taken at the same time, from the same position. It is believed Louisa Bott committed suicide in this location by hanging, when the building was operating as a poor farm.

Below is a photograph taken with a full-spectrum camera by team leader Scott Kenner from Superior, Wisconsin. It shows a spirit occupying the rocking chair in the haunted house experience basement of the François Hotel building, in Redwood Falls, Minnesota.

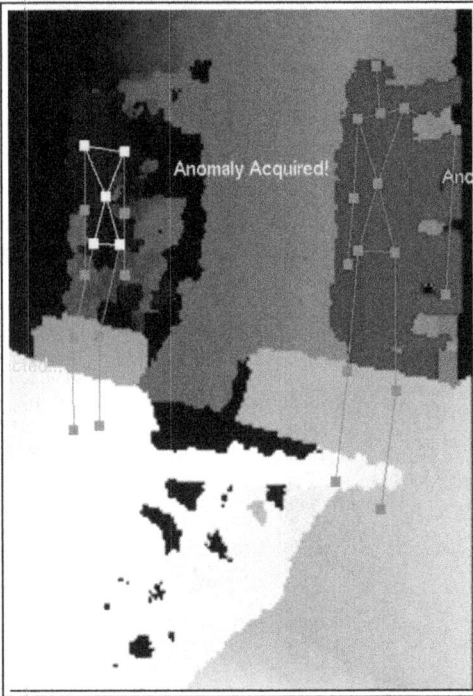

On the left is a photograph taken by Adam Hyatt of Marion, Iowa, with an SLS camera, in the old Delhi schoolhouse building in the grounds of the Redwood Falls Museum. The SLS camera works by finding humanoid areas of articulation based on EMF energy that is manifesting. It shows two spirit children standing mischievously on their desks.

A second photograph was then taken (below) of a spirit child standing next to the teacher's desk.

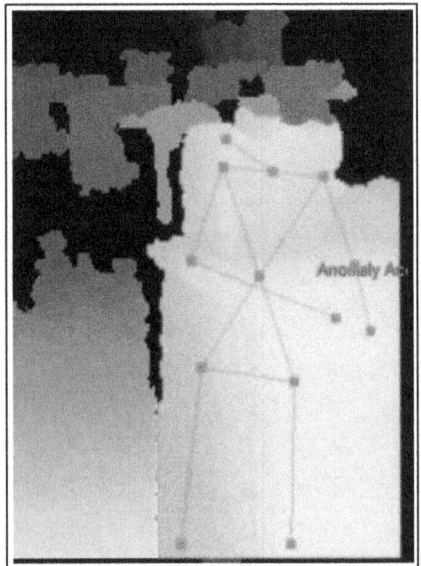

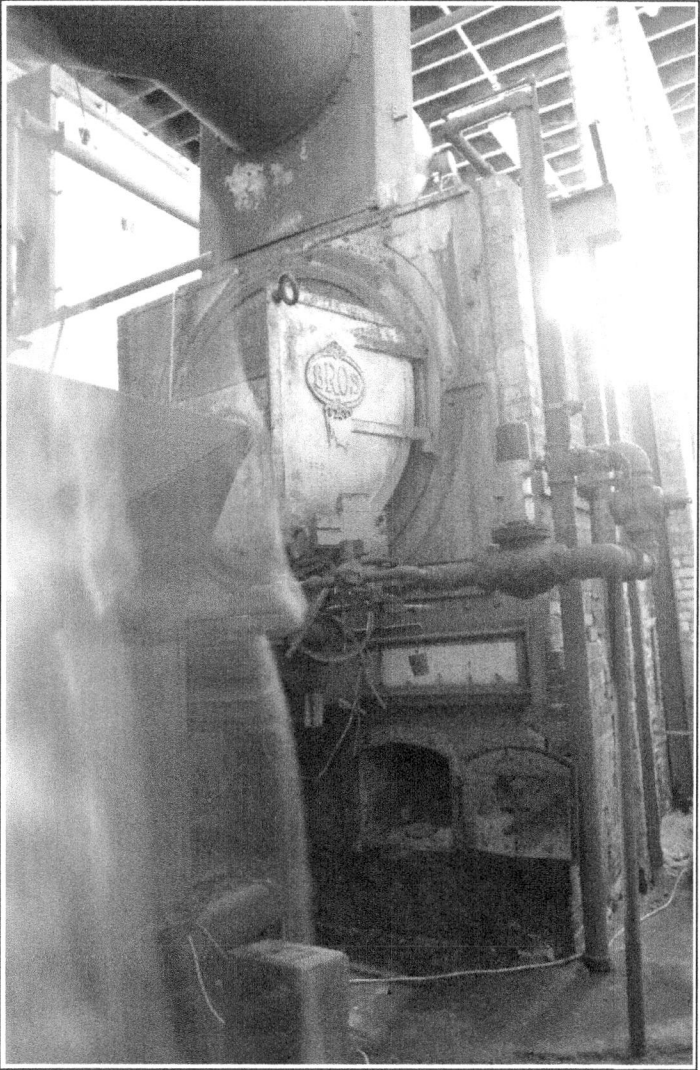

This photograph of a ghost was taken in the furnace room of the Soap Factory in Minneapolis. Due to the limited light at this location the photograph was taken with a tripod and a prolonged exposure time. This allowed for the capture of the movement of the ghost across the picture from left to right. It is see-through but also exhibits a diaphanous nature and a definitive edge.